AF198979

Impressum
Verlag: BABADADA GmbH, Nedderfeld 112 , 22529 Hamburg
Geschäftsführer / Verlagsleitung: Harald Hof
Druck: Books on Demand GmbH, In de Tarpen 42, 22848 Norderstedt

Imprint
Publisher: BABADADA GmbH, Nedderfeld 112 , 22529 Hamburg, Germany
Managing Director / Publishing direction: Harald Hof
Print: Books on Demand GmbH, In de Tarpen 42, 22848 Norderstedt

school
skool

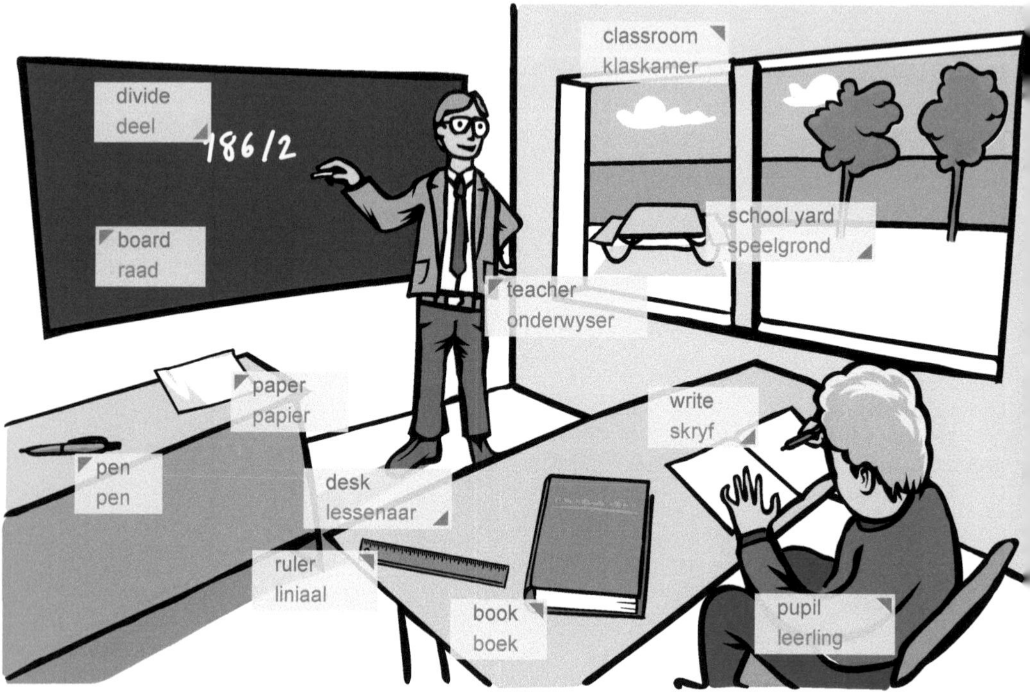

classroom
klaskamer
divide
deel
186/2
board
raad
school yard
speelgrond
teacher
onderwyser
paper
papier
write
skryf
pen
pen
desk
lessenaar
ruler
liniaal
book
boek
pupil
leerling

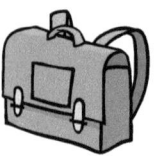

satchel

skooltas

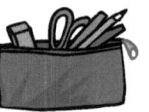

pencil case

potloodhouer

pencil

potlood

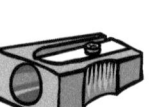

pencil sharpener

skerpmaker

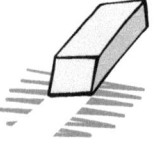

rubber

rubber

drawing pad

tekenblok

drawing

tekening

paintbrush

verfkwas

paint box

verfoppervlak

scissors

skêr

glue

gom

exercise book

oefenboek

homework

huiswerk

number

aantal

add

optel

subtract

aftrek

multiply

maal

calculate

bereken

letter

brief

alphabet

alaphabet

word

woord

text
....
teks

read
....
lees

chalk
....
kryt

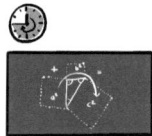

lesson
....
les

register
....
registreer

examination
....
eksamen

certificate
....
sertifikaat

school uniform
....
skooluniform

education
....
onderwys

encyclopedia
....
ensiklopedie

university
....
universiteit

microscope
....
mikroskoop

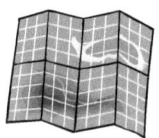

map
....
kaart

waste-paper basket
....
vullisdrom

hotel
hotel

hostel
hostel

ROOMS

currency exchange office
bureau de change

ЄCHANGE

car
motor

language

taal

yes / no

ja / nee

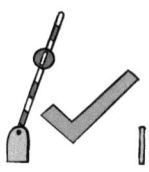

Okay

Goed

hello

hallo

translator

vertaler

Thank you

Dankie

how much is...?

hoeveel is...?

I don´t get it

Ek verstaan nie

problem

probleem

Good evening!

Goeie naand!

Good morning!

Goeie môre!

Good night!

Goeie nag!

goodbye

totsiens

direction

rigting

luggage

bagasie

bag

sak

backpack

rugsak

guest

gas

room

kamer

sleeping bag

slaapsak

tent

tent

tourist information	beach	credit card
toeriste-inligting	strand	kredietkaart

breakfast	lunch	dinner
ontbyt	middagete	aandete

Ticket	elevator	stamp
kaartjie	hysbak	posseël

border	customs	embassy
grens	doeane	ambassade

visa	passport	
visum	paspoort	

transport
vervoer

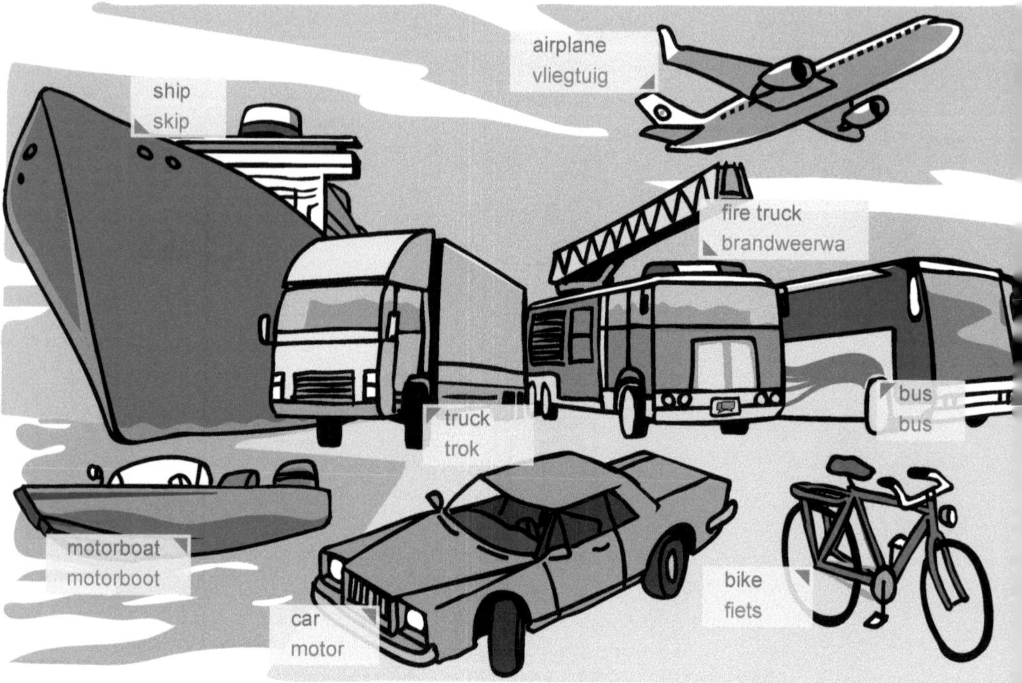
airplane
vliegtuig
ship
skip
fire truck
brandweerwa
bus
bus
truck
trok
motorboat
motorboot
bike
fiets
car
motor

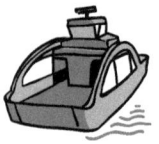

ferry

veerboot

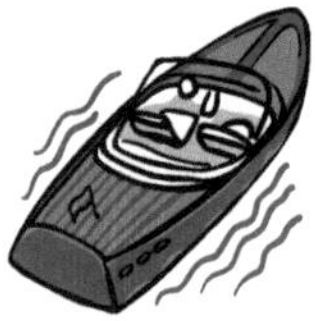

boat

boot

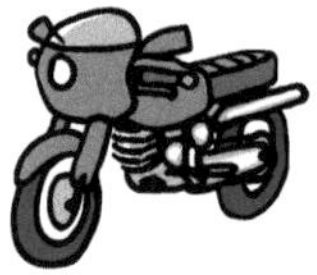

motorbike

motorfiets

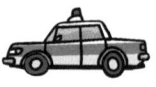

police car

polisiemotor

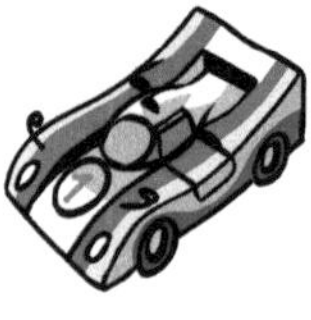

racing car

renmotor

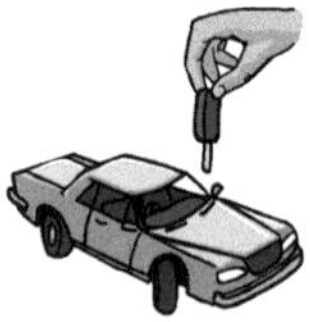

rental car

huurmotor

car sharing

car-sharing

tow truck

insleepvoertuig

garbage truck

vullisverwydering

engine

enjin

fuel

brandstof

fuel station

vulstasie

traffic sign

verkeersteken

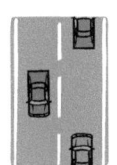

traffic

verkeer

traffic jam

verkeersknoop

parking lot

parkeerplek

train station

stasie

tracks

spore

train

trein

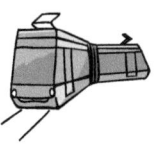

tram

tram

wagon

wa

transport - vervoer

helicopter

helikopter

airport

lughawe

tower

toring

passenger

passasier

container

houer

carton

karton

cart

karretjie

basket

mandjie

take off / land

opstyg / land

city

stad

village

dorpie

city center

middestad

house

huis

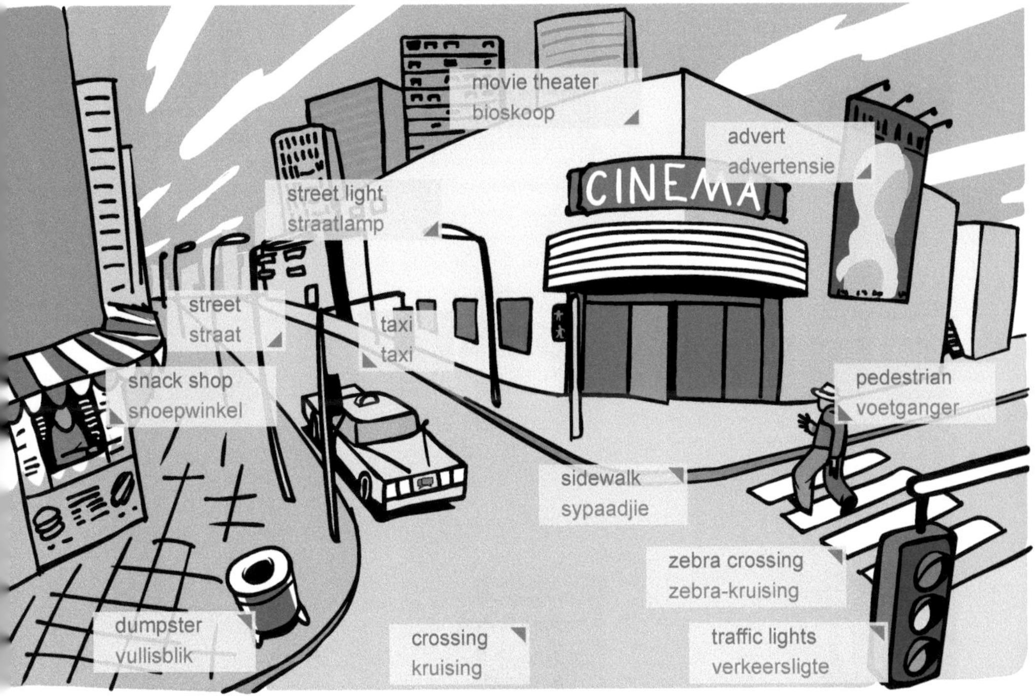

movie theater
bioskoop

advert
advertensie

street light
straatlamp

CINEMA

street
straat

taxi
taxi

snack shop
snoepwinkel

pedestrian
voetganger

sidewalk
sypaadjie

zebra crossing
zebra-kruising

dumpster
vullisblik

crossing
kruising

traffic lights
verkeersligte

hut

hut

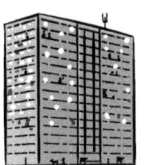

apartment

woonstel

train station

stasie

city hall

stadsaal

museum

museum

school

skool

university
universiteit

bank
bank

hospital
hospitaal

hotel
hotel

pharmacy
apteek

office
kantoor

book shop
boekwinkel

shop
winkel

flower shop
bloemis

supermarket
supermark

market
mark

department store
handelshuis

fishmonger's shop
viswinkel

mall
inkopiesentrum

harbor
hawe

park
park

bench
bankie

bridge
brug

stairs
trappe

subway
moltrein

tunnel
tonnel

bus stop
bushalte

bar
kroeg

restaurant
restaurant

postbox
posbus

street sign
straatnaambord

parking meter
parkeermeter

zoo
dieretuin

swimming pool
swembad

mosque
moskee

farm
plaas

pollution
besoedeling

cemetery
begraafplaas

church
kerk

playground
speelgrond

temple
tempel

landscape
landskap

signpost
padwyser

path
pad

meadow
weiland

stone
klip

hiker
voetslaner

tree
boom

river
rivier

grass
gras

flower
blom

valley
vallei

hill
heuwel

lake
meer

forest
bos

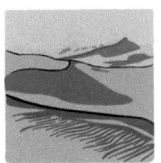

desert
woestyn

volcano
vulkaan

castle
kasteel

rainbow
reënboog

mushroom
sampioen

palm tree
palmboom

mosquito
muskiet

fly
vlieg

ant
mier

bee
by

spider
spinnekop

landscape - landskap

beetle

miskruier

frog

padda

squirrel

eekhoring

hedgehog

krimpvarkie

hare

haas

owl

uil

bird

voël

swan

swaan

boar

wildevark

deer

takbok

moose

elk

dam

opgaardam

wind turbine

windturbine

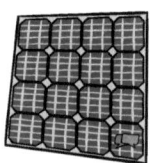

solar panel

sonpaneel

climate

klimaat

waiter
kelner

menu
menu

chair
stoel

soup
sop

pizza
pizza

tablecloth
tafeldoek

cutlery
eetgerei

starter
voorgereg

main course
hoofgereg

dessert
nagereg

drinks
drankies

food
kos

bottle
bottel

fast food

kitskos

street food

straatkos

teapot

teepot

sugar bowl

suikerverpakking

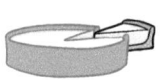

portion

porsie

espresso machine

espresso masjien

high chair

hoë stoel

bill

rekening

tray

skinkbord

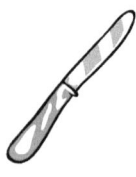

knife

mes

fork

vurk

spoon

lepel

teaspoon

teelepel

serviette

servet

glass

glas

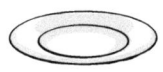

plate
gereg

soup plate
sopbakkie

saucer
piering

sauce
sous

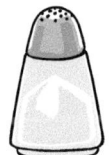

salt shaker
soutpot

pepper mill
pepermeul

vinegar
asyn

oil
olie

spices
speserye

ketchup
tamatiesous

mustard
mosterd

mayonnaise
mayonaise

supermarket
supermark

special offer
spesiale aanbieding
FOR
customer
kliënt
dairy products
suiwelprodukte
fruit
vrugte
shopping cart
trollie

BUTCHERS

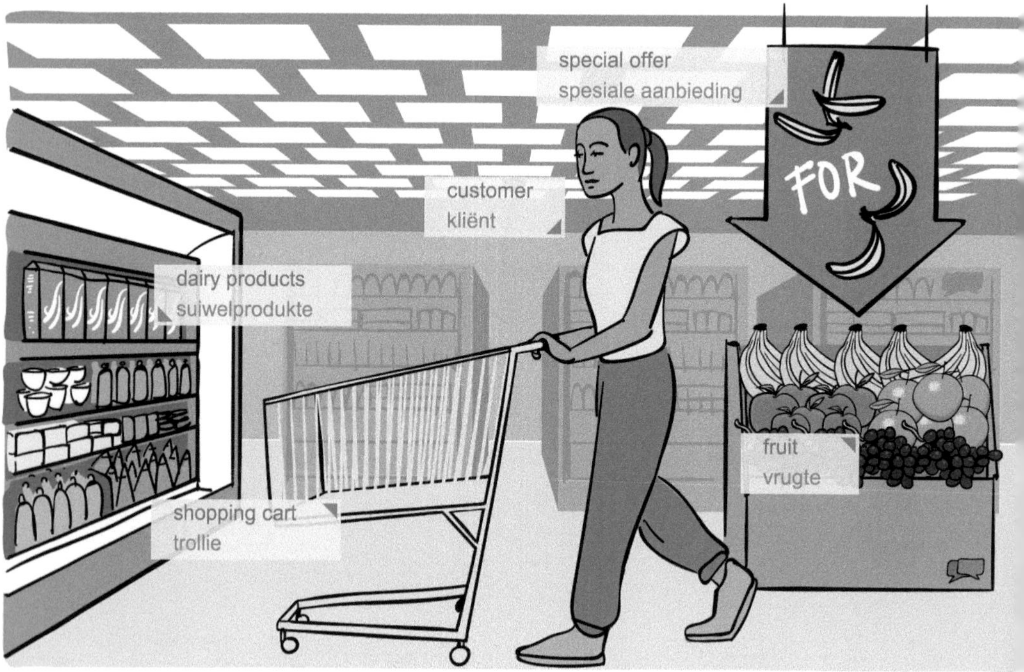

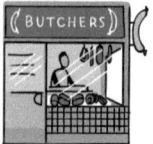

butcher's shop

slaghuis

BAKERY

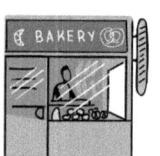

bakery

bakkery

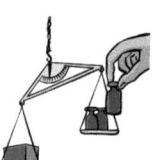

weigh

weeg

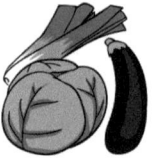

vegetables

groente

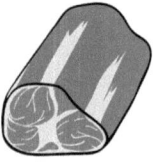

meat

vleis

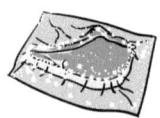

frozen food

bevrore voedsel

cold cuts
kouevleis

canned food
blikkieskos

detergent
waspoeier

candy
lekkers

household products
huishoudelike produkte

cleaning products
skoonmaakprodukte

sales representative
verkoopsvrou

cash register
kasregister

cashier
kassier

shopping list
inkopielys

opening hours
besigheidsure

wallet
beursie

credit card
kredietkaart

bag
sak

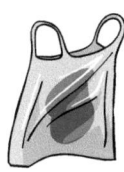

plastic bag
plastieksak

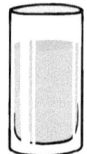

water

water

juice

sap

milk

melk

coke

coke

wine

wyn

beer

bier

alcohol

alkohol

cocoa

kakao

tea

tee

coffee

koffie

espresso

espresso

cappuccino

cappuccino

banana

piesang

apple

appel

orange

lemoen

melon

waatlemoen

lemon

suurlemoen

carrot

wortel

garlic

knoffel

bamboo

bamboes

onion

ui

mushroom

sampioen

nuts

neute

noodles

noedels

spaghetti

spaghetti

rice

rys

salad

slaai

fries

aartappelskyfies

fried potatoes

gebraaide aartappels

pizza

pizza

hamburger

hamburger

sandwich

toebroodjie

escalope

kotelet

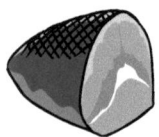

ham

ham

salami

salami

sausage

wors

chicken

hoender

roast

braaivleis

fish

vis

porridge oats

hawermoutflokkies

muesli

muesli

cornflakes

graanvlokkies

flour

meel

croissant

croissant

bread roll

broodrolletjie

bread

brood

toast

roosterbrood

cookies

koekies

butter

botter

curd

dikmelk

cake

koek

egg

eier

fried egg

gebraaide eier

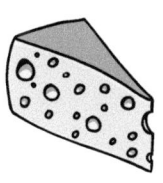

cheese

kaas

ice cream

roomys

sugar

suiker

honey

heuning

jelly

konfyt

nougat cream

nougat-smeer

curry

kerrie

farm
plaas

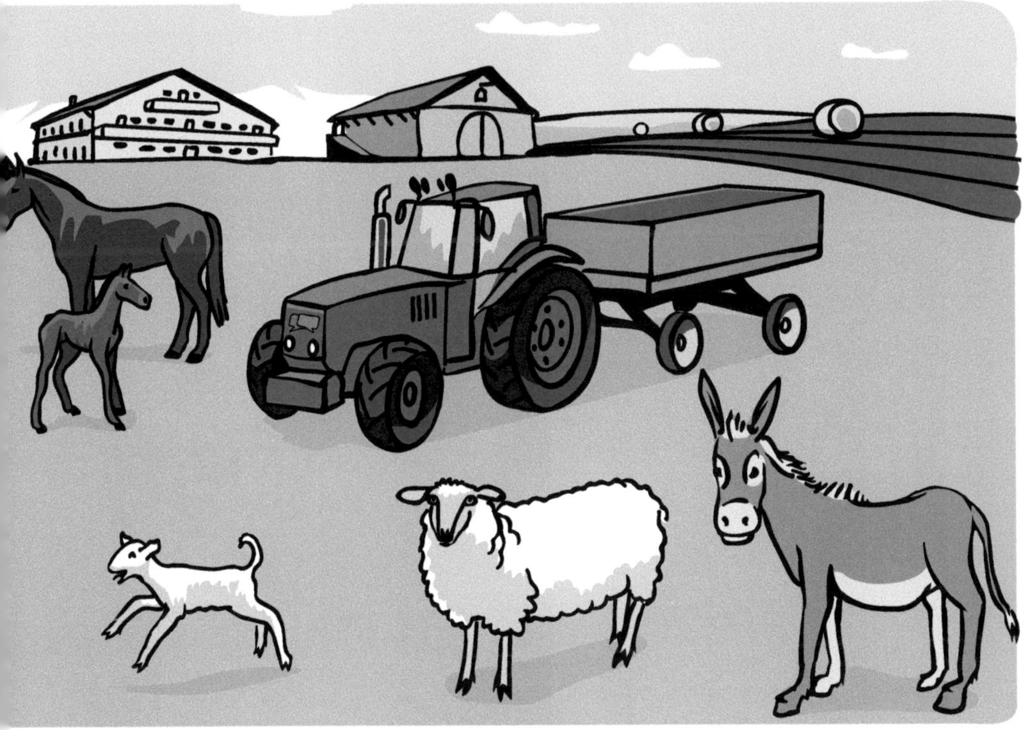

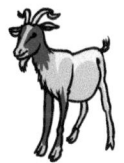

goat

bok

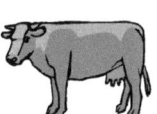

cow

koei

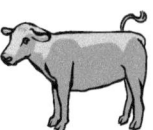

calf

kalf

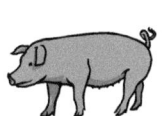

pig

vark

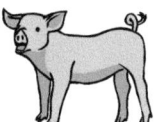

piglet

varkie

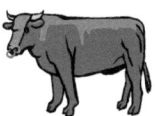

bull

bul

goose

gans

duck

eend

chick

kuiken

hen

hen

cockerel

haan

rat

rot

cat

kat

mouse

muis

ox

os

dog

hond

dog house

hondehok

garden hose

tuinslang

watering can

gieter

scythe

sens

plow

ploeg

sickle

sekel

hoe

skoffel

pitchfork

gaffel

axe

byl

pushcart

kruiwa

trough

trog

milk can

melkkan

sack

sak

fence

heining

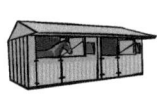

stable

stal

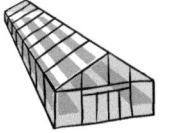

greenhouse

kweekhuis

soil

grond

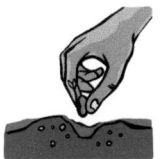

seed

saad

fertilizer

kunsmis

combine harvester

stroper

harvest
oes

harvest
oes

yams
yam

wheat
koring

soya
soja

potato
aartappel

corn
koring

rapeseed
raapsaad

fruit tree
vrugteboom

manioc
broodwortel

grain
graan

house
huis

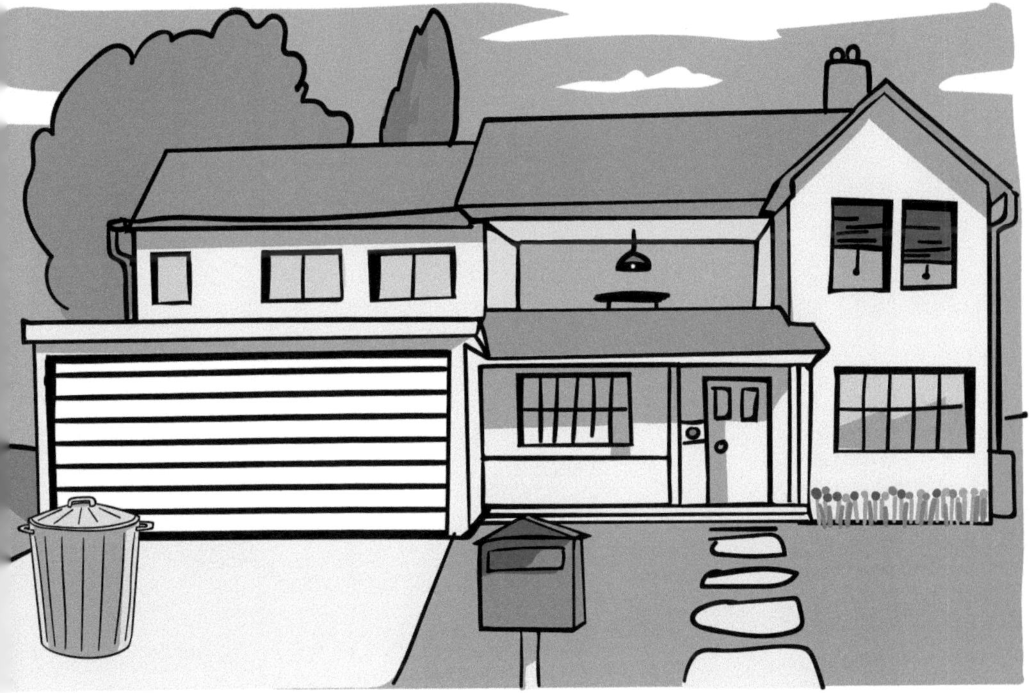

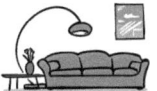

living room
woonkamer

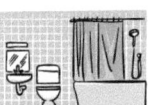

bathroom
badkamer

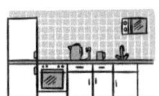

kitchen
kombuis

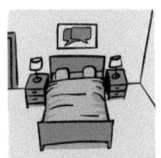

bedroom
slaapkamer

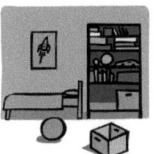

kids room
kinderkamer

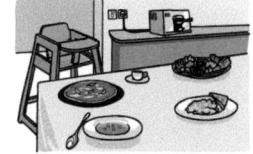

dining room
eetkamer

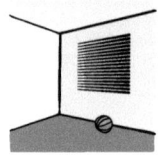

floor
....
vloer

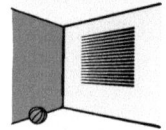

wall
....
muur

ceiling
....
plafon

cellar
....
kelder

sauna
....
sauna

balcony
....
balkon

terrace
....
terras

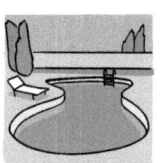

pool
....
swembad

lawn mower
....
grassnyer

sheet
....
beddegoedoortreksel

bedspread
....
deken

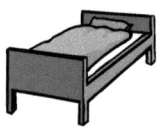

bed
....
bed

broom
....
besem

bucket
....
emmer

switch
....
skakelaar

living room
woonkamer

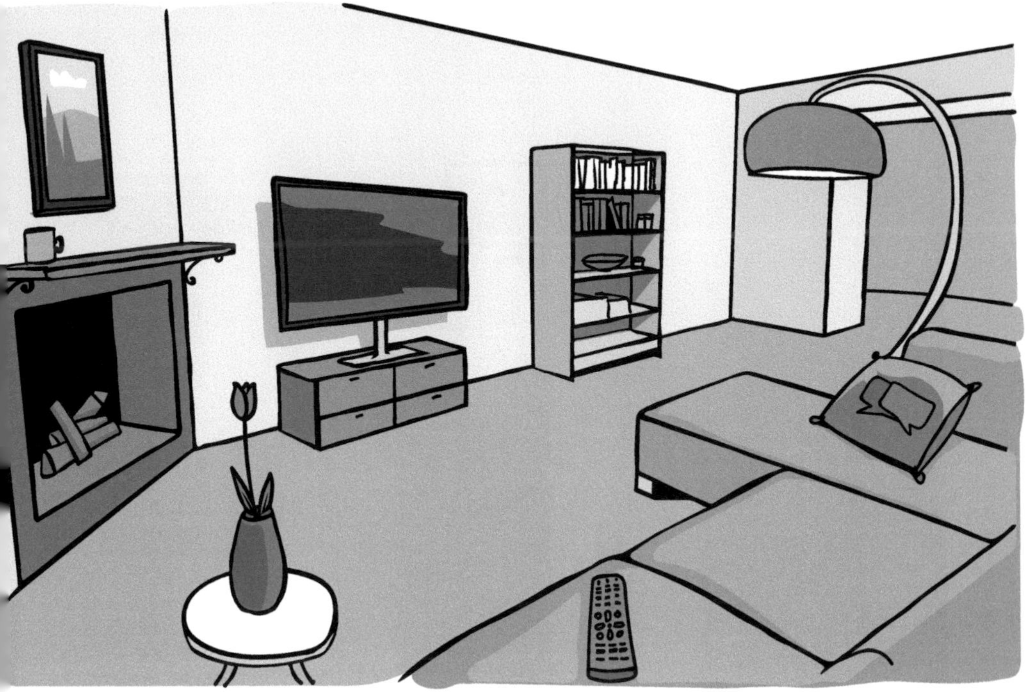

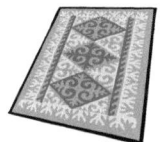

carpet

mat

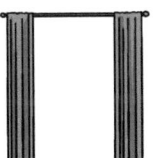

drape

gordyn

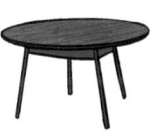

table

tafel

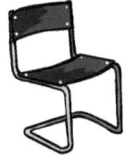

chair

stoel

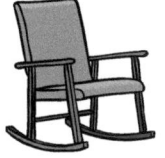

rocking chair

wiegstoel

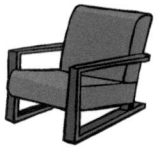

armchair

leunstoel

book boek	blanket kombers	decoration versiering

firewood vuurmaakhout	film film	stereo system hoëtroustel

key sleutel	newspaper koerant	painting skildery

poster plakkaat	radio radio	notebook notaboekie

vacuum cleaner stofsuier	cactus kaktus	candle kers

kitchen
kombuis

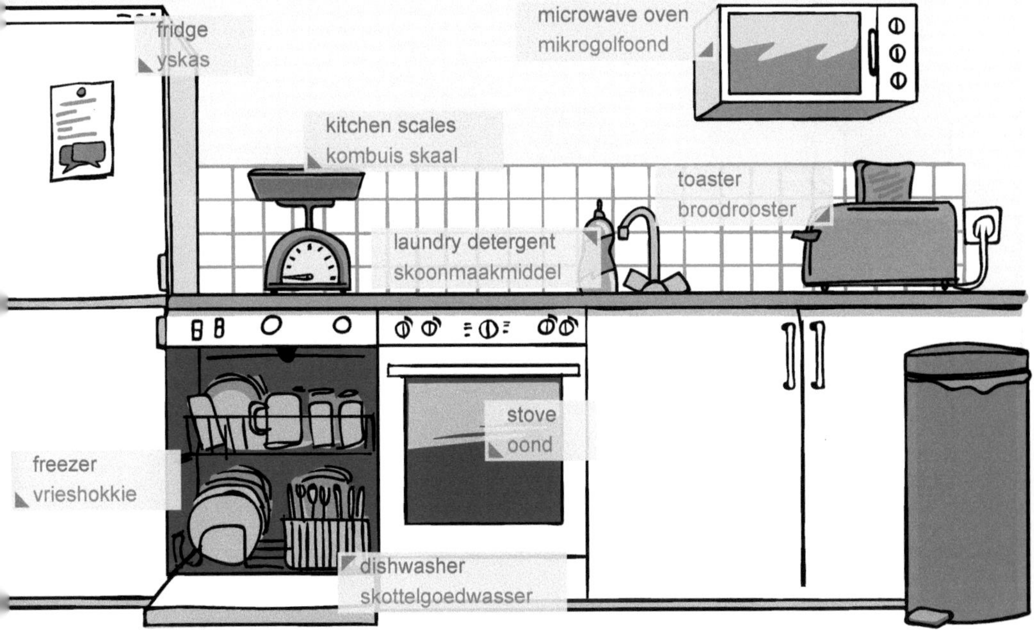

fridge
yskas
microwave oven
mikrogolfoond
kitchen scales
kombuis skaal
toaster
broodrooster
laundry detergent
skoonmaakmiddel
stove
oond
freezer
vrieshokkie
dishwasher
skottelgoedwasser

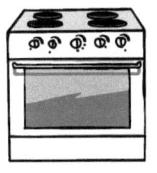

cooker

drukkoker

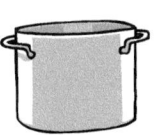

pot

pot

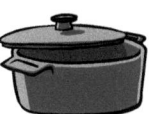

cast-iron pot

ysterpot

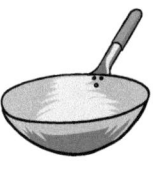

wok / kadai

wok / kadai

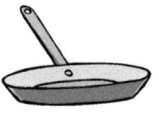

pan

pan

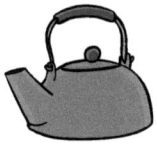

kettle

ketel

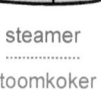

steamer

stoomkoker

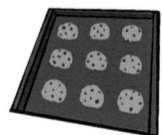

baking tray

bakplaat

crockery

breekware

mug

beker

bowl

bak

chopsticks

eetstokkie

ladle

skeplepel

spatula

spatel

whisk

klitser

strainer

sif

sieve

sif

grater

rasper

mortar

vysel

barbecue

braai

fireplace

oop vuur

chopping board

broodplank

rolling pin

koekroller

corkscrew

kurktrekker

can

kan

can opener

blikoopmaker

oven cloth

vatlap

sink

opwasbak

brush

borsel

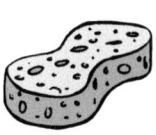

sponge

spons

blender

menger

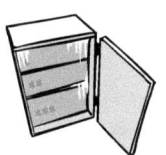

deep freezer

vrieskas

baby bottle

bababottel

tap

kraan

kitchen - kombuis

bathroom
badkamer

heating
verwarming
towel
handdoek
shower
stort
shower curtain
stortgordyn
bubble bath
borrel bad
bathtub
bad
glass
glas
washing machine
wasmasjien
tap
kraan
tiles
teëls
potty
potjie
sink
opwasbak

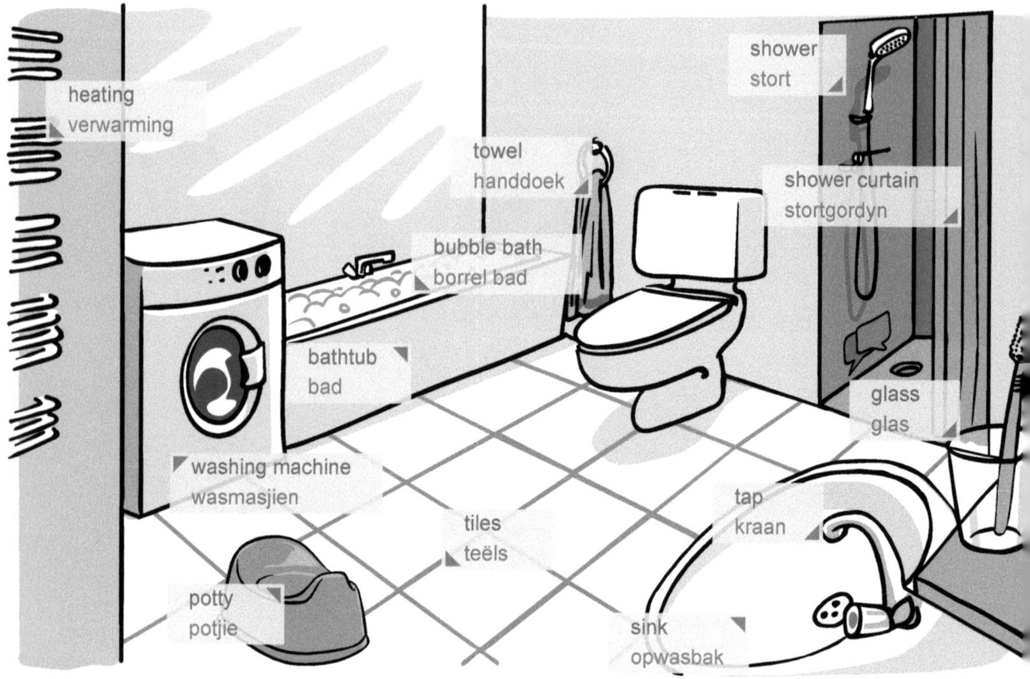

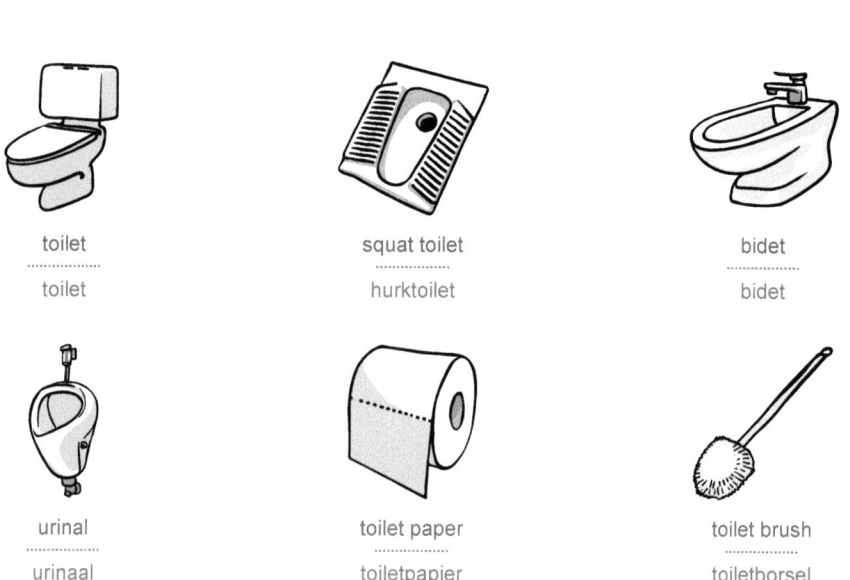

toilet
toilet

squat toilet
hurktoilet

bidet
bidet

urinal
urinaal

toilet paper
toiletpapier

toilet brush
toiletborsel

toothbrush

tandeborsel

toothpaste

tandepasta

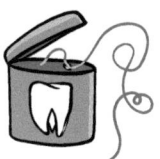

dental floss

tande vlos

wash

was

hand shower

handstort

douche

stort

basin

wasbak

back brush

rugkantborsel

soap

seep

shower gel

stortgel

shampoo

sjampoe

flannel

flanel

drain

drein

creme

room

deodorant

reukweerder

mirror

spieël

hand mirror

spieëltjie

razor

skeermes

shaving foam

skeerroom

aftershave

naskeermiddel

comb

kam

brush

borsel

hair-dryer

haardroër

hairspray

haarsproei

makeup

grimmering

lipstick

lipstifie

nail varnish

naellak

cotton wool

watte

nail scissors

naelknipper

perfume

parfuum

washbag

toiletsakkie

stool

stoel

weighing scales

skaal

bathrobe

badjas

rubber gloves

rubberhandskoene

tampon

tampon

sanitary towel

sanitêre handdoek

chemical toilet

chemiese toilet

kids room
kinderkamer

alarm clock
wekker
cuddly toy
snoesige speelding
toy car
speelgoedkarretjie
rattle
ratel
doll's house
pophuis
present
geskenk

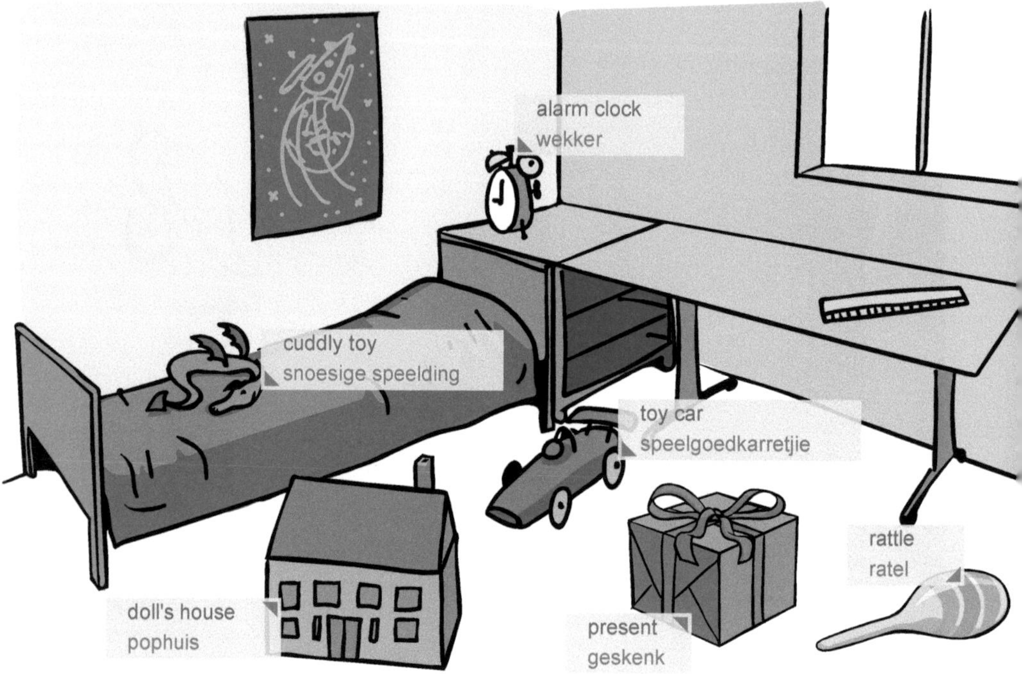

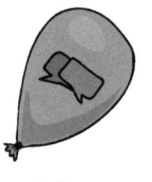

balloon

ballon

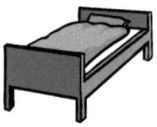

bed

bed

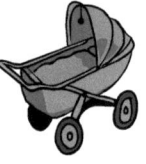

stroller

stootwaentjie

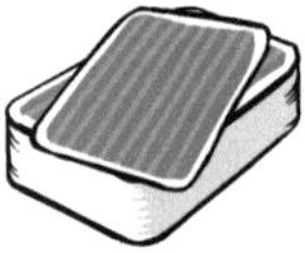

deck of cards

kaartespel

jigsaw

legkaart

SUPER
MEGA

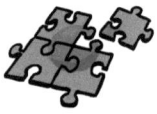

comic

tekenprent

lego bricks

lego-blokkies

toy blocks

speelgoedblokke

action figure

animasieheld

romper suit

groeipakkie

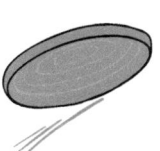

frisbee

frisbee

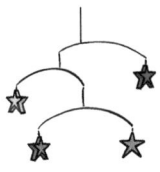

mobile

mobile

board game

bordspeletjie

dice

dobbelsteen

model train set

model trein stel

pacifier

fopspeen

party

partytjie

picture book

prenteboek

ball

bal

doll

pop

play

speel

sandpit

sandput

swing

swaai

toys

speelgoed

video game console

videospeletjie-konsole

tricycle

driewiel

teddy bear

teddiebeer

wardrobe

klerekas

clothing

klere

socks

sokkies

stockings

kouse

tights

broekiekouse

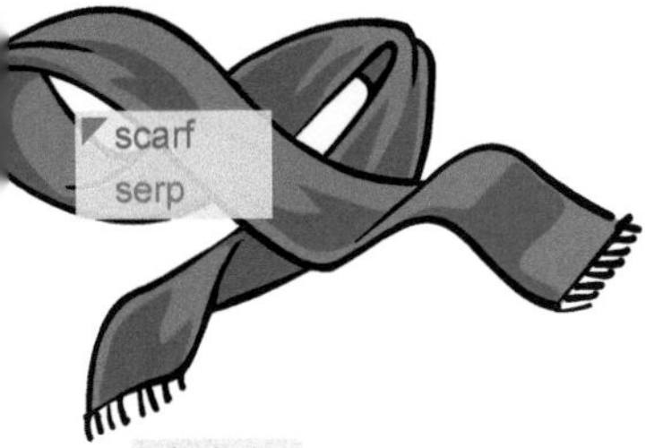

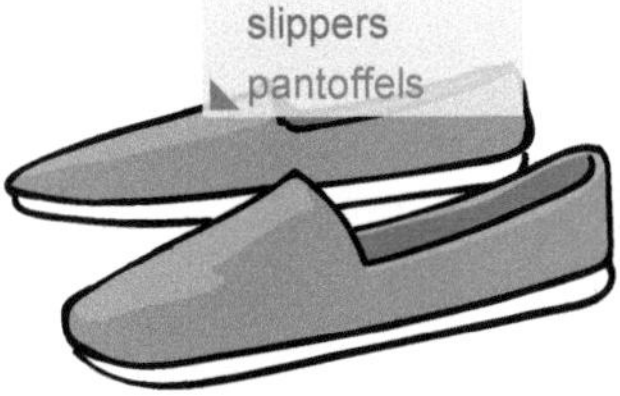

scarf
serp

umbrella
sambreel

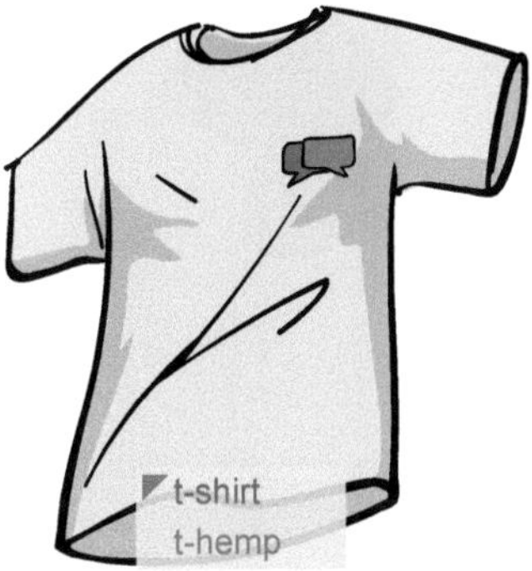

t-shirt
t-hemp

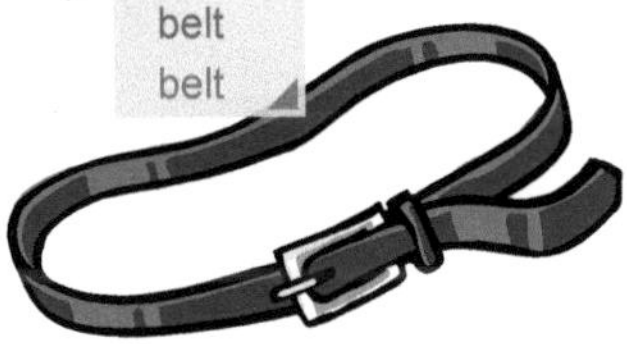

belt
belt

boots
skoene

slippers
pantoffels

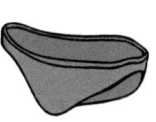
sneakers
tekkies

sandals
....
sandale

shoes
....
skoene

rubber boots
....
rubber stewels

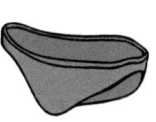
underwear
....
onderbroek

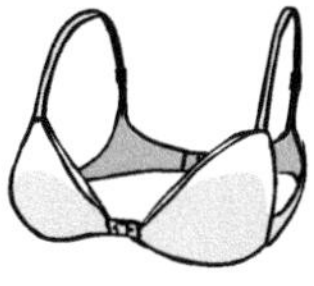

bra
....
bra

undershirt
....
onderbaadjie

clothing - klere

45

body

liggaam

pants

broek

jeans

jeans

skirt

romp

blouse

bloes

shirt

hemp

pullover

oortrektrui

sweater

oortrektrui

blazer

baadjie

jacket

baadjie

coat

jas

raincoat

reënjas

costume

kostuum

dress

rok

wedding dress

trourok

suit

pak

nightgown

nagrok

pajamas

pajamas

sari

sari

headscarf

kopdoek

turban

tulband

burka

burqa

kaftan

kaftan

abaya

abaya

swimsuit

swembroek

trunks

swembroek

shorts

kortbroek

tracksuit

sweetpak

apron

voorskoot

gloves

handskoene

clothing - klere

button
knoppie

glasses
bril

bracelet
armband

necklace
halssnoer

ring
ring

earring
oorbel

cap
pet

coat hanger
klerehanger

hat
hoed

tie
das

zip
rits

helmet
helmet

braces
draadjies

school uniform
skooluniform

uniform
uniform

bib
....
bib

pacifier
....
fopspeen

diaper
....
doek

office
kantoor

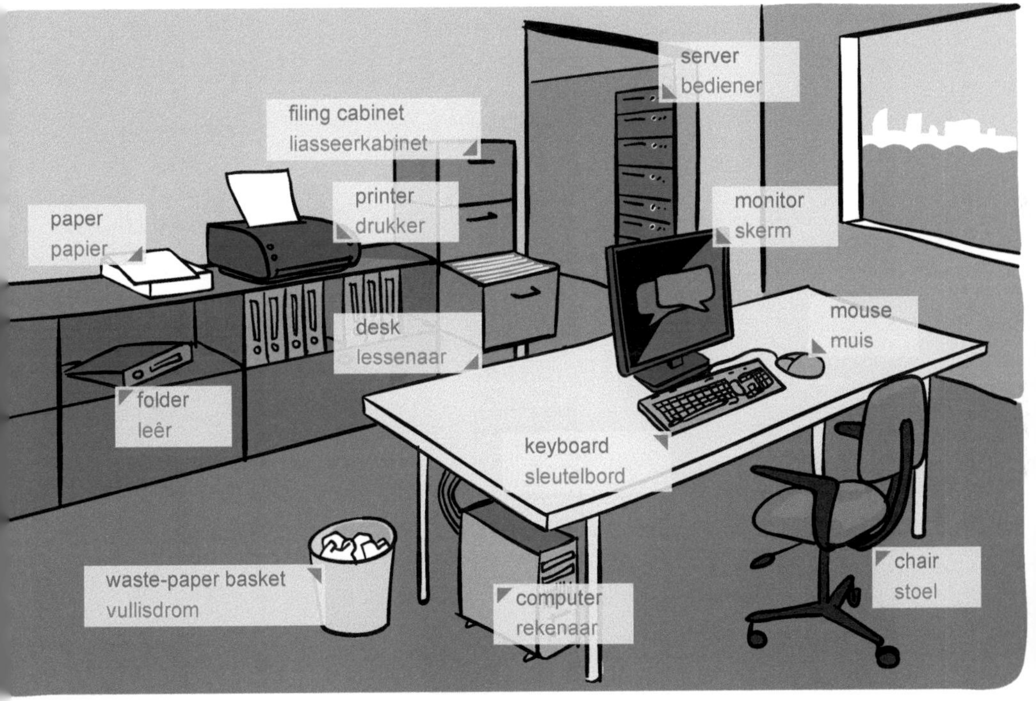

server
bediener

filing cabinet
liasseerkabinet

printer
drukker

monitor
skerm

paper
papier

desk
lessenaar

mouse
muis

folder
leêr

keyboard
sleutelbord

waste-paper basket
vullisdrom

computer
rekenaar

chair
stoel

coffee mug
....
koffiebeker

calculator
....
sakrekenaar

internet
....
internet

laptop

skootrekenaar

letter

brief

message

boodskap

cell phone

selfoon

network

netwerk

photocopier

fotostaatmasjien

software

sagteware

telephone

telefoon

plug socket

muurprop

fax machine

faksmasjien

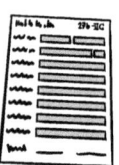

form

vorm

document

dokument

buy

koop

pay

betaal

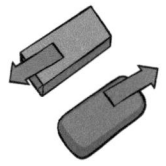

trade

besigheid doen

money

geld

 **USD**

dollar

dollar

 **EUR**

euro

euro

 **JPY**

yen

yen

 **RUB**

rouble

roebel

 **CHF**

Swiss franc

switserse frank

 **CNY**

renminbi yuan

renminbi yuan

 **INR**

rupee

rupee

cash point

kontantteller (ATM)

currency exchange office

bureau de change

gold

goud

silver

silwer

oil

olie

energy

energie

price

prys

contract

kontrak

tax

belasting

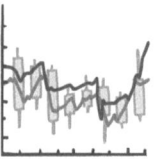

stock

aandele

work

werk

employee

werknemer

employer

werkgewer

factory

fabriek

shop

winkel

police officer
polisiebeampte

fireman
brandweerman

cook
kok

doctor
dokter

pilot
vlieënier

gardener

tuinier

carpenter

timmerman

seamstress

naaldwerkster

judge

regter

chemist

chemikus

actor

akteur

bus driver

busbestuurder

taxi driver

taxibestuurder

fisherman

visserman

cleaning lady

skoonmaakvrou

roofer

dakwerker

waiter

kelner

hunter

jagter

painter

skilder

baker

bakker

electrician

elektrisiën

builder

bouer

engineer

ingenieur

butcher

slagter

plumber

loodgieter

postman

posman

soldier

soldaat

architect

argitek

cashier

kassier

florist

bloemiste

hairdresser

haarkapper

conductor

kondukteur

mechanic

werktuigkundige

captain

kaptein

dentist

tandarts

scientist

wetenskaplike

rabbi

rabbi

imam

imam

monk

monnik

pastor

predikant

tools
gereedskap

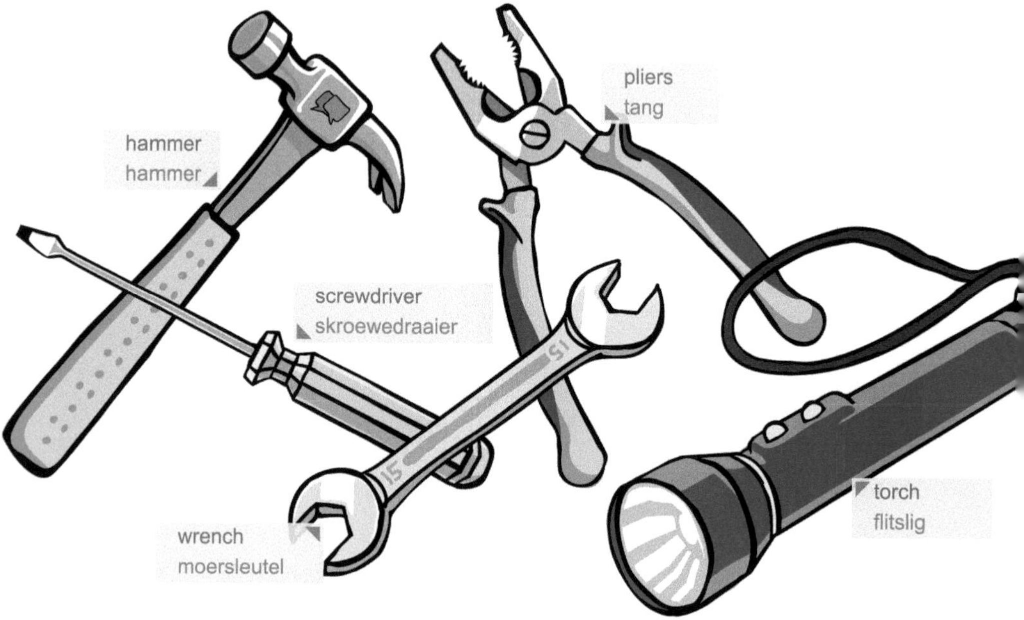

hammer
hammer
pliers
tang
screwdriver
skroewedraaier
wrench
moersleutel
torch
flitslig

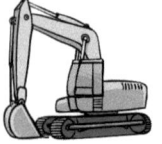

excavator

graaftoestel

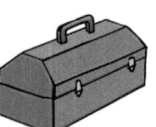

toolbox

gereedskapskis

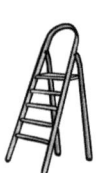

ladder

leer

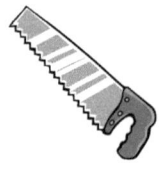

saw

saag

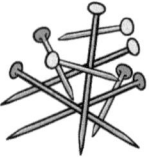

nails

naels

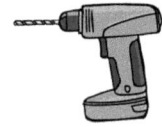

drill

boor

repair
regmaak

shovel
graaf

Damn!
verdomp!

dustpan
skoppie

paint can
verfpot

screws
skroewe

musical instruments
musiekinstrumente

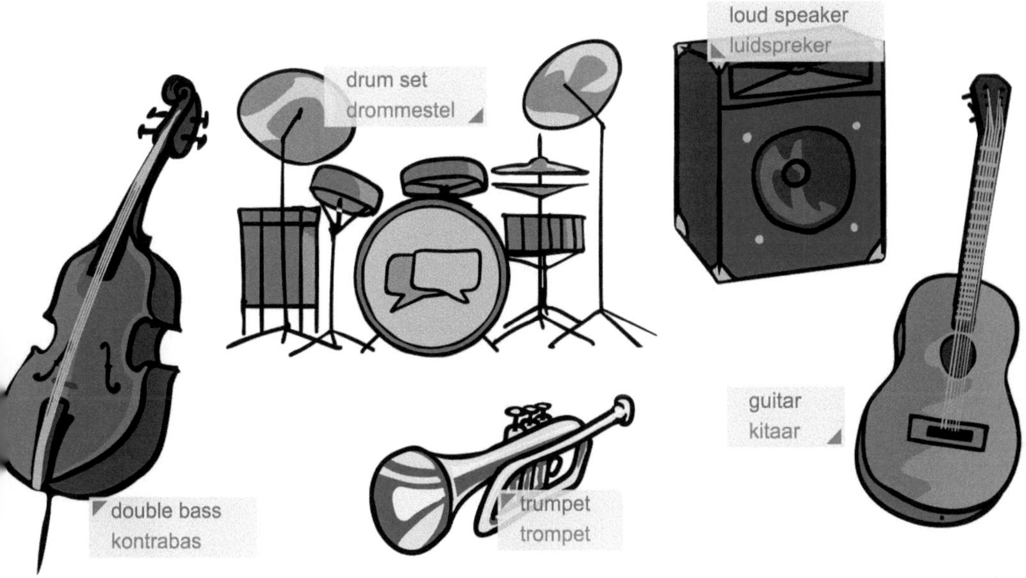

drum set
drommestel

loud speaker
luidspreker

guitar
kitaar

double bass
kontrabas

trumpet
trompet

piano

klavier

violin

viool

bass

bas

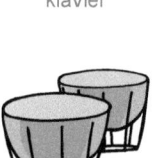

timpani

keteltrom

drums

dromme

keyboard

sleutelbord

saxophone

saksofoon

flute

fluit

microphone

mikrofoon

zoo
dieretuin

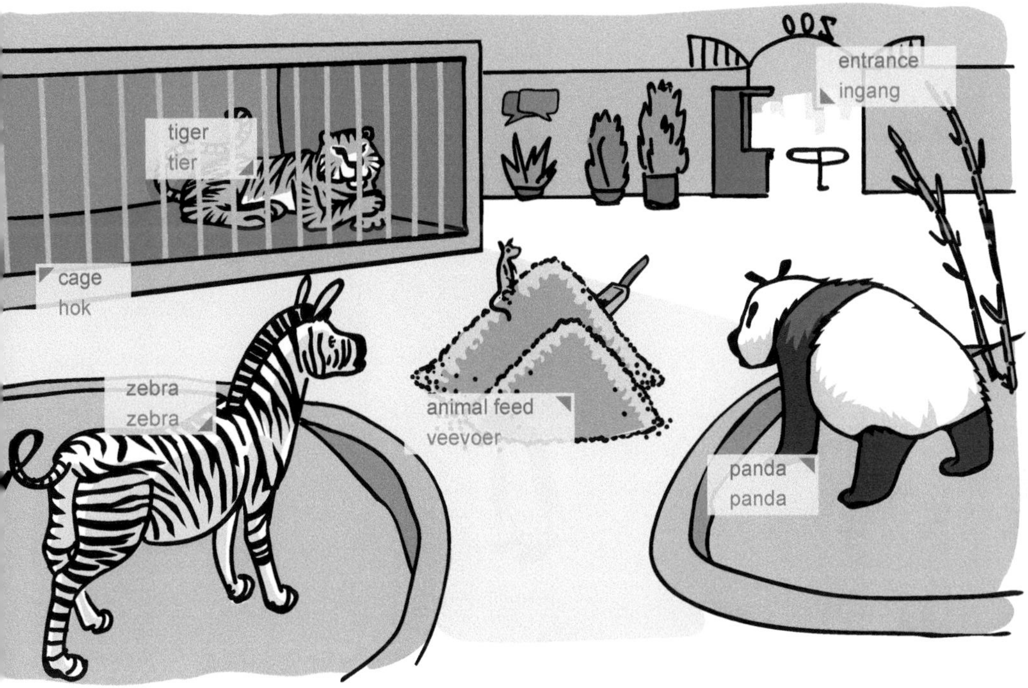
tiger
tier
entrance
ingang
cage
hok
zebra
zebra
animal feed
veevoer
panda
panda

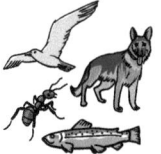

animals
diere

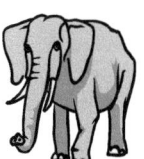

elephant
olifant

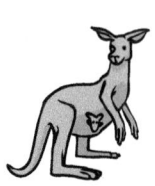

kangaroo
kangaroo

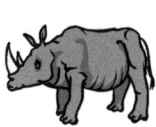

rhino
renoster

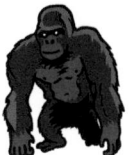

gorilla
gorilla

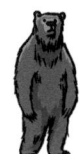

bear
beer

camel

kameel

ostrich

volstruis

lion

leeu

monkey

aap

flamingo

flamink

parrot

papegaai

polar bear

ysbeer

penguin

pikkewyn

shark

haai

peacock

pou

snake

slang

crocodile

krokodil

zookeeper

dieretuinopsigter

seal

rob

jaguar

jaguar

pony
ponie

leopard
luiperd

hippo
seekoei

giraffe
kameelperd

eagle
arend

boar
wildevark

fish
vis

turtle
skilpad

walrus
walrus

fox
jakkals

gazelle
gemsbok

American football
Amerikaanse Voetbal

cycling
fietsry

tennis
tennis

basketball
basketbal

swimming
swem

boxing
boks

ice hockey
ys-hokkie

soccer
sokker

badminton
pluimbal

athletics
atletiek

handball
handbal

skiing
ski

polo
polo

activities
aktiwiteite

jump
spring
hug
drukkie
laugh
lag
walk
loop
sing
sing
dream
droom
pray
bid
kiss
soen

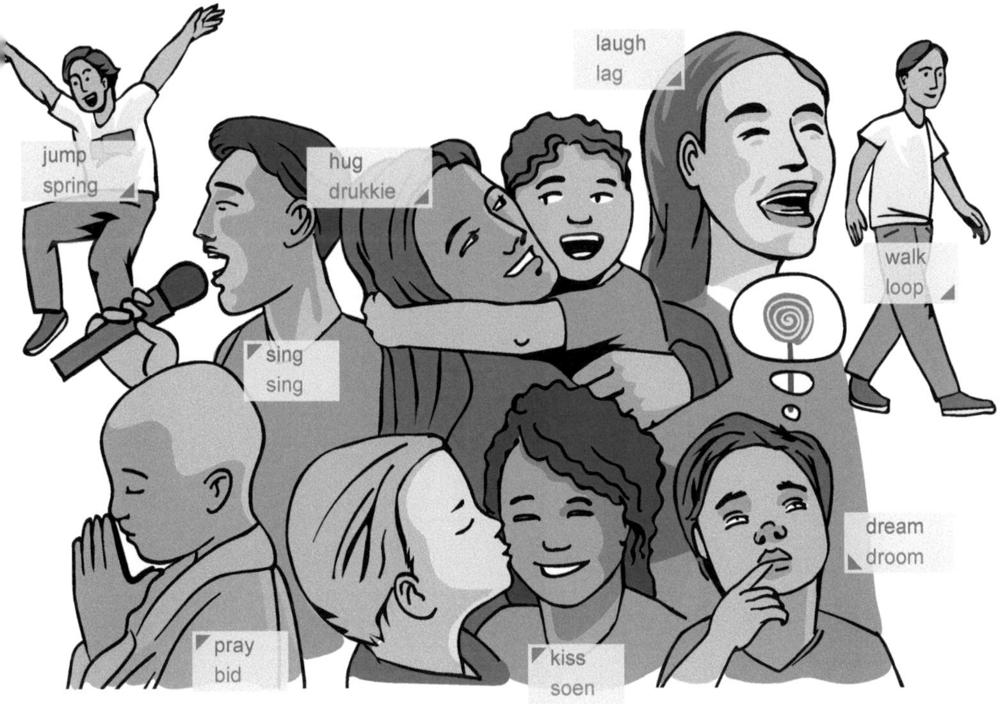

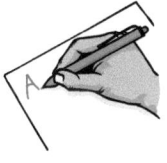

write
skryf

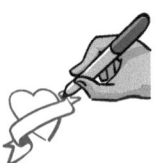

draw
teken

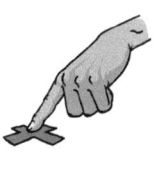

show
show

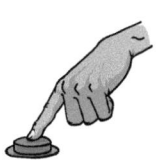

push
druk

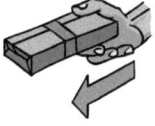

give
gee

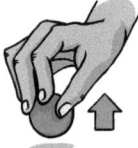

take
neem

have
het

do
doen

be
wees

stand
staan

run
hardloop

pull
trek

throw
gooi

fall
val

lie
jok

wait
wag

carry
dra

sit
sit

get dressed
aantrek

sleep
slaap

wake up
wakker word

look at

kyk na

cry

huil

stroke

streel

comb

kam

talk

praat

understand

verstaan

ask

vra

listen

luister

drink

drink

eat

eet

tidy up

opruim

love

liefhê

cook

kook

drive

ry

fly

vlieg

activities - aktiwiteite

sail
seil

calculate
bereken

read
lees

learn
leer

work
werk

marry
trou

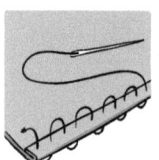

sew
naai

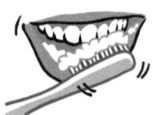

brush teeth
tande borsel

kill
doodmaak

smoke
rook

send
stuur

family

familie

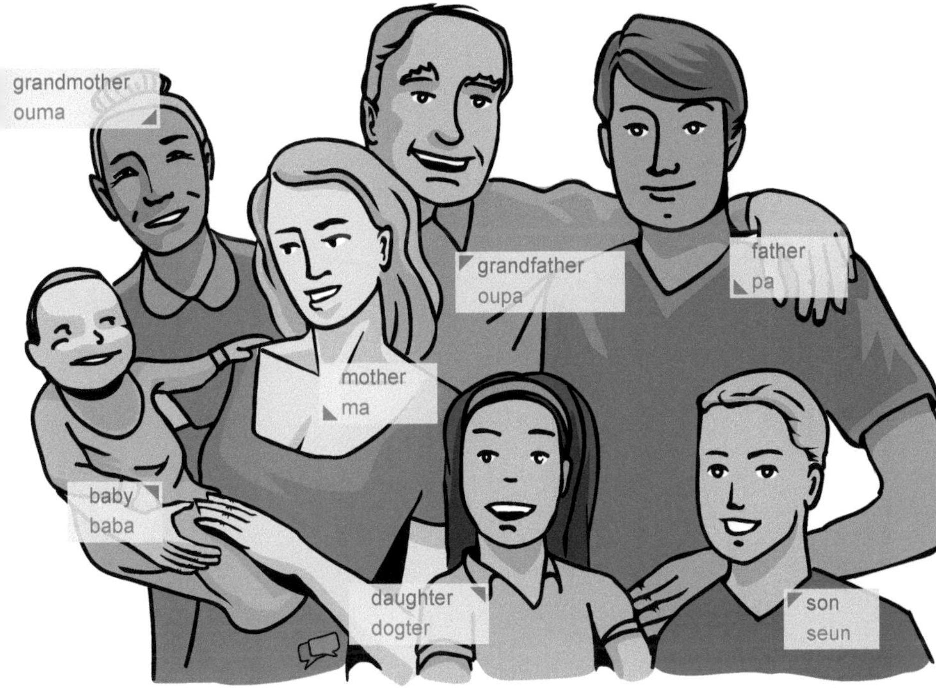
grandmother
ouma
grandfather
oupa
father
pa
mother
ma
baby
baba
daughter
dogter
son
seun

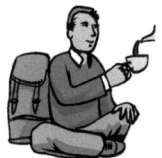

guest

gas

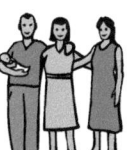

aunt

tannie

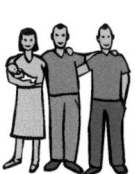

uncle

oom

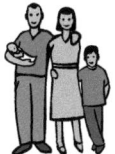

brother

broer

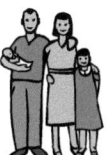

sister

suster

body
liggaam

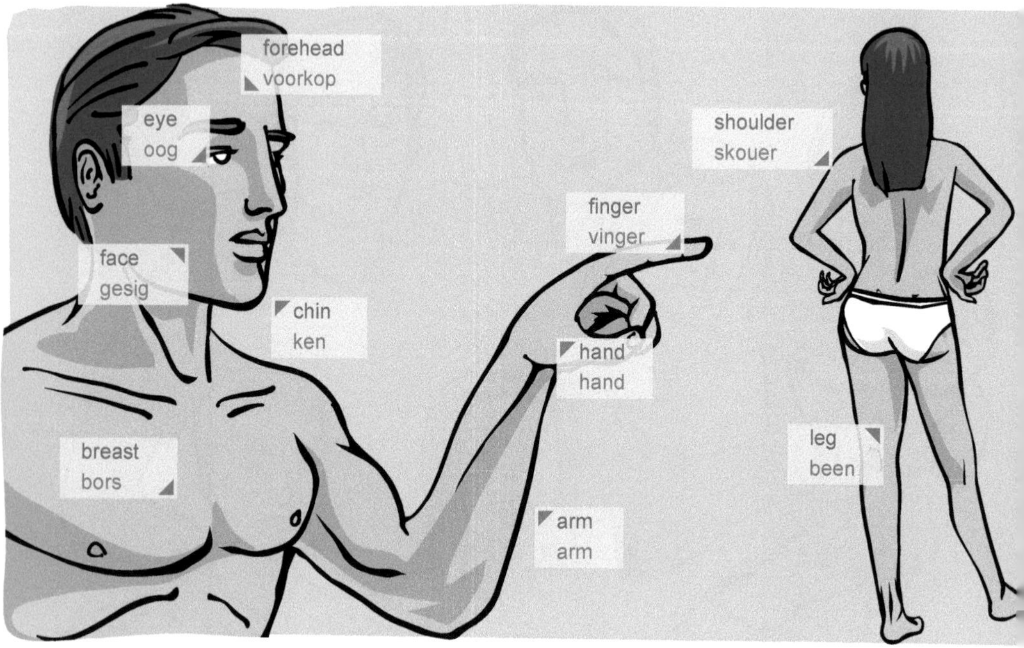

forehead
voorkop

eye
oog

shoulder
skouer

finger
vinger

face
gesig

chin
ken

hand
hand

breast
bors

leg
been

arm
arm

baby
baba

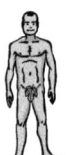

man
man

woman
vrou

girl
meisie

boy
seun

head
kop

back
....
rug

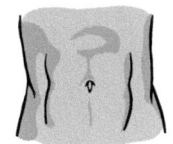

belly
....
buik

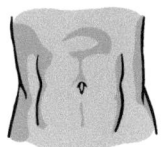

navel
....
naelstring

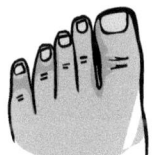

toe
....
toon

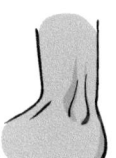

heel
....
hak

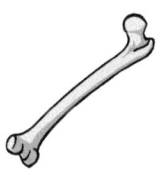

bone
....
been

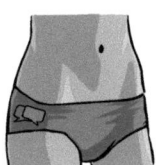

hip
....
heup

knee
....
knie

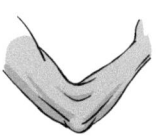

elbow
....
elmboog

nose
....
neus

buttocks
....
boude

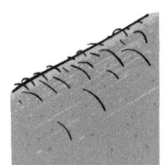

skin
....
vel

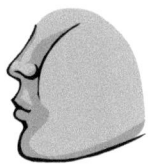

cheek
....
wang

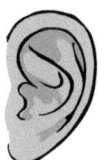

ear
....
oor

lip
....
lippe

mouth

mond

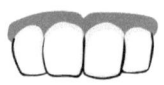

tooth

tand

tongue

tong

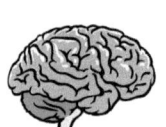

brain

brein

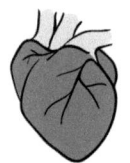

heart

hart

muscle

spiere

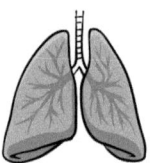

lung

long

liver

lewer

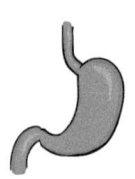

stomach

maag

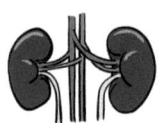

kidneys

niere

sex

seks

condom

kondoom

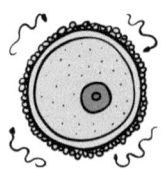

ovum

eierstok

semen

semen

pregnancy

swangerskap

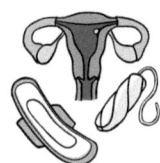

menstruation
menstruasie

vagina
vagina

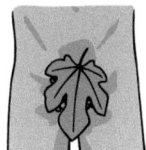

penis
penis

eyebrow
wenkbrou

hair
hare

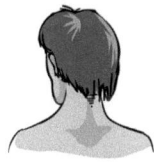

neck
nek

hospital
hospitaal

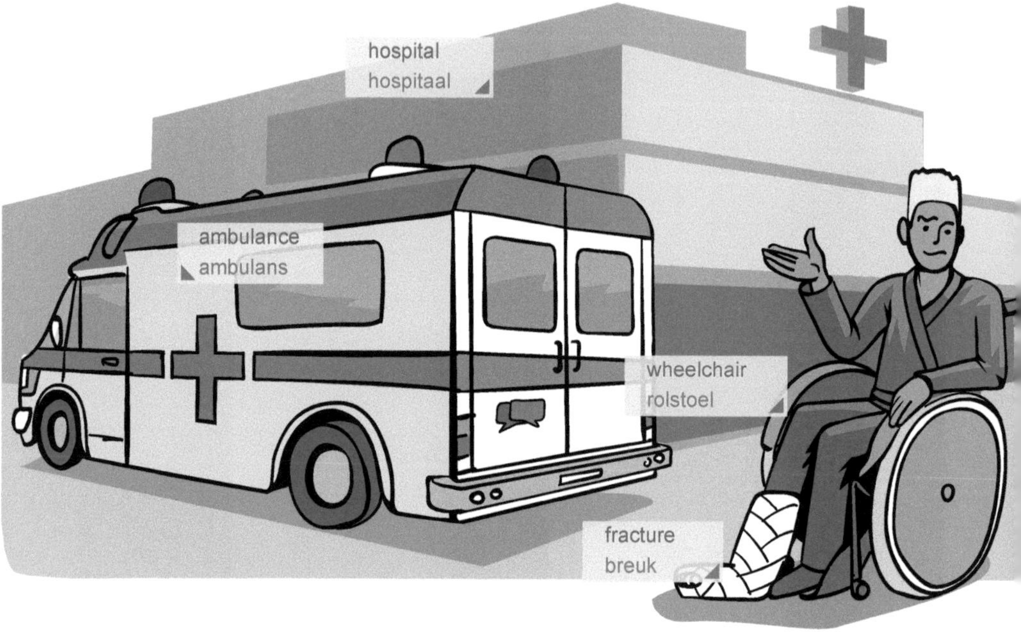

hospital
hospitaal
ambulance
ambulans
wheelchair
rolstoel
fracture
breuk

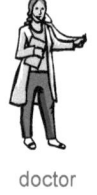

doctor

dokter

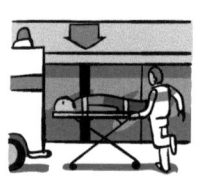

emergency room

ongevalle

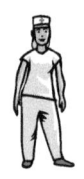

nurse

verpleegster

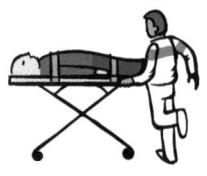

emergency

noodgeval

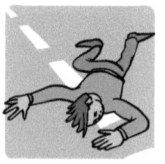

unconscious

bewusteloos

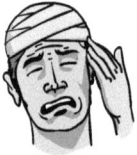

pain

pyn

injury

besering

bleeding

bloeding

heart attack

hartaanval

stroke

beroerte

allergy

allergie

cough

hoes

fever

koors

flu

griep

diarrhea

diarree

headache

hoofpyn

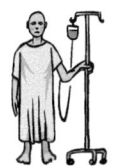

cancer

kanker

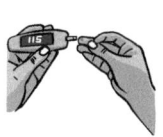

diabetes

diabetes

surgeon

chirurg

scalpel

skalpel

operation

operasie

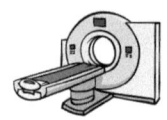

CT

CT

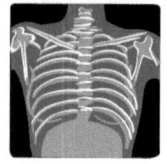

x-ray

X-straal

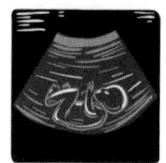

ultrasound

ultraklank

face mask

gesigmasker

disease

siekte

waiting room

wagkamer

crutch

kruk

plaster

gips

bandage

verband

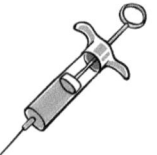

injection

inspuiting

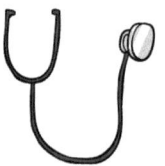

stethoscope

stetoskoop

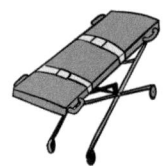

stretcher

draagbaar

clinical thermometer

kliniese termometer

birth

geboorte

overweight

oorgewig

hearing aid

gehoorapparaat

disinfectant

ontsmettingsmiddel

infection

infeksie

virus

virus

HIV / AIDS

MIV / vigs

medicine

medisyne

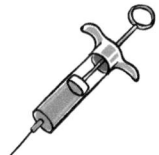

vaccination

inenting

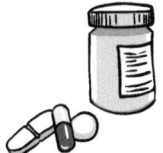

tablets

tablette

pill

pil

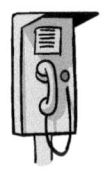

emergency call

noodoproep

blood pressure monitor

blooddrukmonitor

ill / healthy

siek / gesond

Help!

Help!

alarm

alarm

assault

aanranding

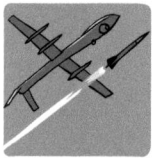

attack

aanval

danger

gevaar

emergency exit

nooduitgang

Fire!

Brand!

fire extinguisher

brandblusser

accident

ongeluk

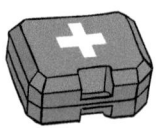

first-aid kit

noodhulpkissie

SOS

SOS

police

polisie

Europe

Europa

North America

Noord-Amerika

South America

Suid-Amerika

Africa

Afrika

Asia

Asië

Australia

Australië

Atlantic

Atlantiese Oseaan

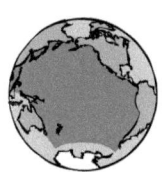

Pacific

Stille Oseaan

Indian Ocean

Indiese Oseaan

Antarctic Ocean

Antarktiese Oseaan

Arctic Ocean

Arktiese Oseaan

North pole

Noordpool

South pole

Suidpool

Antarctica

Antarktika

earth

aarde

land

land

sea

see

island

eiland

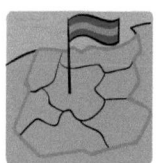

nation

nasie

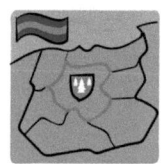

state

staat

earth - aarde

clock face

horlosie

hour hand

uur-aanwyser

minute hand

minuut-aanwyser

second hand

sekonde-aanwyser

What time is it?

Hoe laat is dit?

day

dag

time

tyd

now

nou

digital watch

digitale horlosie

minute

minuut

hour

uur

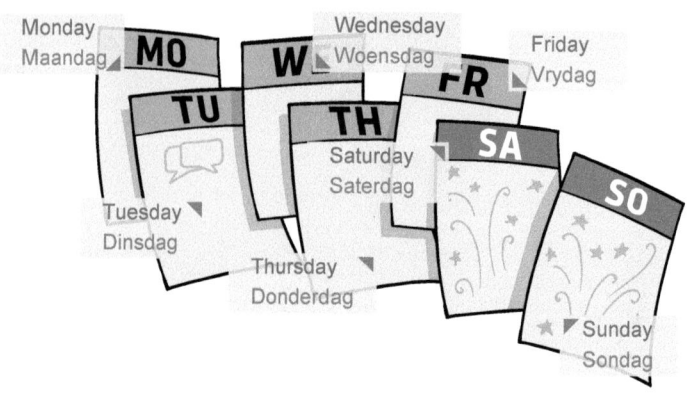

Monday — Maandag — **MO**
Wednesday — Woensdag — **W**
Friday — Vrydag — **FR**
Tuesday — Dinsdag — **TU**
Thursday — Donderdag — **TH**
Saturday — Saterdag — **SA**
Sunday — Sondag — **SO**

yesterday
gister

today
vandag

tomorrow
môre

morning
oggend

noon
middag

evening
aand

workdays
werksdae

weekend
naweek

year
jaar

rain
reën
wind
wind
snow
sneeu
spring
lente
fall
Herfs
summer
somer
winter
winter

4.APRIL 11°
5.APRIL 4°
6.APRIL 13°
7.APRIL 8°
8.APRIL 10°

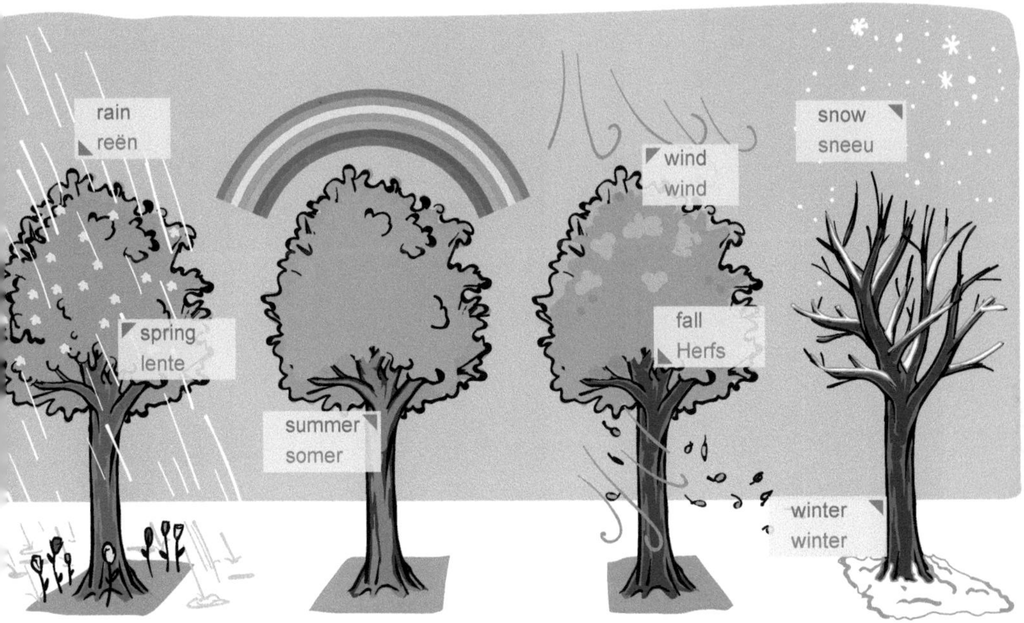

weather forecast

weervoorspelling

F C
120 90 60 30 0 -30
40 30 20 10 0 -10 -20

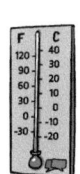

thermometer

termometer

sunshine

sonskyn

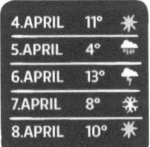

cloud

wolk

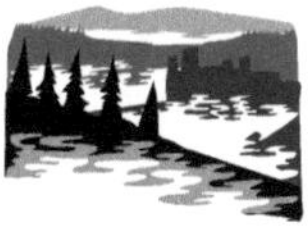

fog

mis

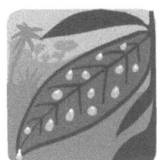

humidity

humiditeit

lightning

weerlig

thunder

donderweer

storm

storm

hail

hael

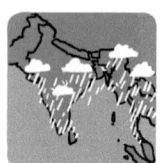

monsoon

reënseisoen

flood

vloed

ice

ys

January

Januarie

February

Februarie

March

Maart

April

April

May

Mei

June

Junie

July

Julie

August

Augustus

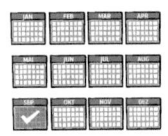

September
September

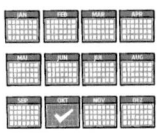

October
Oktober

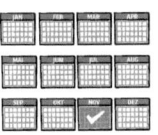

November
November

December
Desember

shapes
vorms

circle
sirkel

square
vierkant

rectangle
reghoek

triangle
driehoek

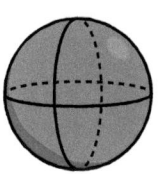

sphere
gebied

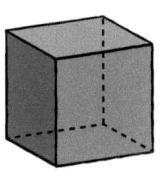

cube
kubus

colors

kleure

white

wit

yellow

geel

orange

oranje

pink

pink

red

rooi

purple

pers

blue

blou

green

groen

brown

bruin

gray

grys

black

swart

a lot / a little

'n baie / 'n bietjie

angry / calm

kwaad / kalm

beautiful / ugly

pragtig / lelik

beginning / end

begin / einde

big / small

groot / klein

bright / dark

helder / donker

brother / sister

broer / suster

clean / dirty

skoon / vuil

complete / incomplete

volledige / onvolledige

day / night

dag / nag

dead / alive

dood / lewendig

wide / narrow

wyd / smal

edible / inedible

eetbare / oneetbaar

evil / kind

kwaad / vriendelik

excited / bored

opgewonde / verveeld

fat / thin

vet / maer

first / last

eerste / laaste

friend / enemy

vriend / vyand

full / empty

vol / leeg

hard / soft

hard / sag

heavy / light

swaar / lig

hunger / thirst

honger / dors

ill / healthy

siek / gesond

illegal / legal

onwettige / wettige

intelligent / stupid

slim / dom

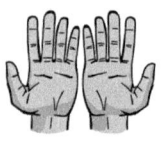

left / right

links / regs

near / far

naby / vêr

opposites - teenoorgesteldes

new / used

nuut / tweedehands

nothing / something

niks / iets

old / young

oud / jonk

on / off

aan / af

open / closed

oop / toe

quiet / loud

stil / lawaaierig

rich / poor

ryk / arm

right / wrong

reg / verkeerd

rough / smooth

grof / glad

sad / happy

hartseer / gelukkig

short / long

kort / lank

slow / fast

stadig / vinnig

wet / dry

nat / droog

warm / cool

warm / koel

war / peace

oorlog / vrede

getalle

0	**1**	**2**
zero	one	two
nul	een	twee
3	**4**	**5**
three	four	five
drie	vier	vyf
6	**7**	**8**
six	seven	eight
ses	sewe	agt
9	**10**	**11**
nine	ten	eleven
nege	tien	elf

12

twelve

twaalf

13

thirteen

dertien

14

fourteen

veertien

15

fifteen

vyftien

16

sixteen

sestien

17

seventeen

sewentien

18

eighteen

agtien

19

nineteen

negentien

20

twenty

twintig

100

hundred

honderd

1.000

thousand

duisend

1.000.000

million

miljoen

tale

English
Engels

American English
Amerikaanse Engels

Chinese Mandarin
Mandaryns

Hindi
Hindi

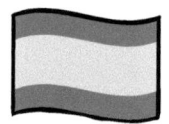

Spanish
Spaans

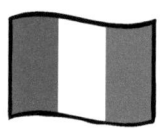

French
Frans

Arabic
Arabies

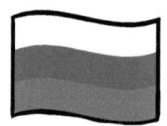

Russian
Russies

Portuguese
Portugees

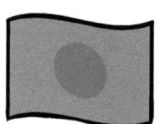

Bengali
Bengaals

German
Duits

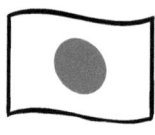

Japanese
Japanees

I

Ek

you

jy

he / she / it

hy / sy / dit

we

ons

you

julle

they

hulle

who?

wie?

what?

wat?

how?

hoe?

where?

waar?

when?

wanneer?

name

naam

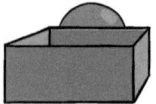

behind

agter

in

in

in front of

voor

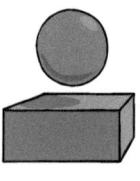

over

oor

on

bo-op

under

onder

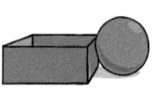

beside

langs

between

tussen

place

plek